LEARNING BISAYA

Let's Go To The Beach

Adto ta sa dagat

BY CATHERINE GAMOLO AGOPCAN

LEARNING BISAYA SERIES

LET'S GO TO THE BEACH (2022)
TIME FOR SCHOOL (COMING SOON)

Today, my Lola (grandmother), Lolo (grandfather), and I are going to the dagat (beach).

Can you help me pack my bolsa (bag)?

Kinahanglan nako kini nga mga butang:
(I will need these items.)

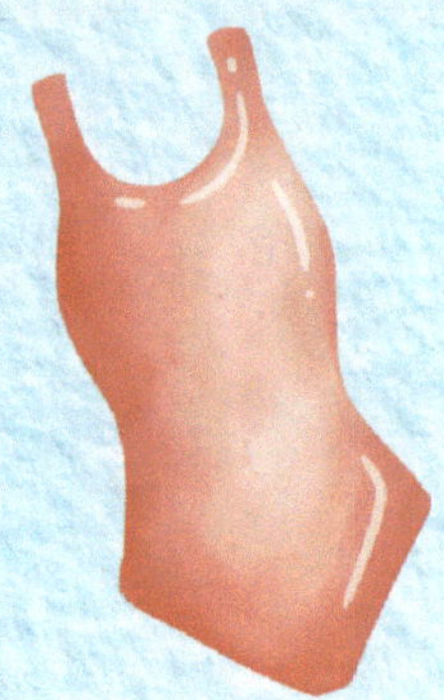

bola
(ball)

gamit sa pangligo
(clothes for swimming)

tsinelas
(slippers)

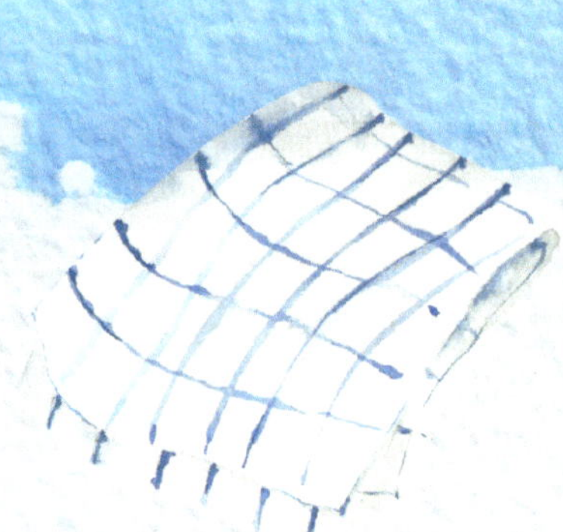

tualya
(towel)

balde para dulaan
(bucket for playing)

kalo
(hat)

And of course, my sunscreen because the adlaw (sun) kusog kaayo (is very strong).

We will pack baon (food) and
habol (blanket).
Mag piknik ta!

Here is the food that we will bring.
Unsa man imong paborito?
(Which one is your favorite?

saging
(banana)

puto
(steamed cake)

suman
(rice cake)

tubig
(water)

kukis
(cookies)

sandwich

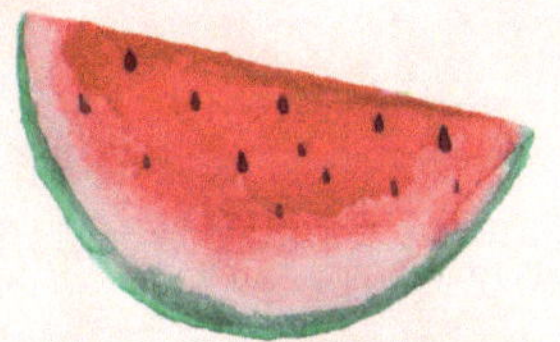

pakwan
(watermelon)

otap
(cookie)

pinya
(pineapple)

mani
(peanuts)

chips

Dad-on ni Lolo ang iyang gitara.
(Lolo will bring his guitar.)

Dad-on ni Lola ang iyang paypay
(Lola will bring her fan.)

Time to get into the kotse (car).
Adto na ta!
(Let's go!)

langgam
(birds)
Na-a na ta!
(We're here!)
payong
(umbrella)

Nindot ang dagat!
(The sea is beautiful!)
alimango
(crab)
tindahan
(store)

Mag set-up ta diri
(Let's set up here.)
tubig
(water)
balas
(sand)

Magdula ta!
(Let's play!)

Nindot ang tubig!
(The water is great!)
kastilyo
(castle)
pala
(shovel)
balde para dulaan
(bucket to play with)

Nakita ba nimo kana?
(Did you see that?)
It's a lumod (dolphin)!
Hi!

Molangoy ta!
(Let's swim!)
pasayan
(shrimp)
isda
(fish)

Daghan ang mga mananap dinhi!
(There are so many animals here!)

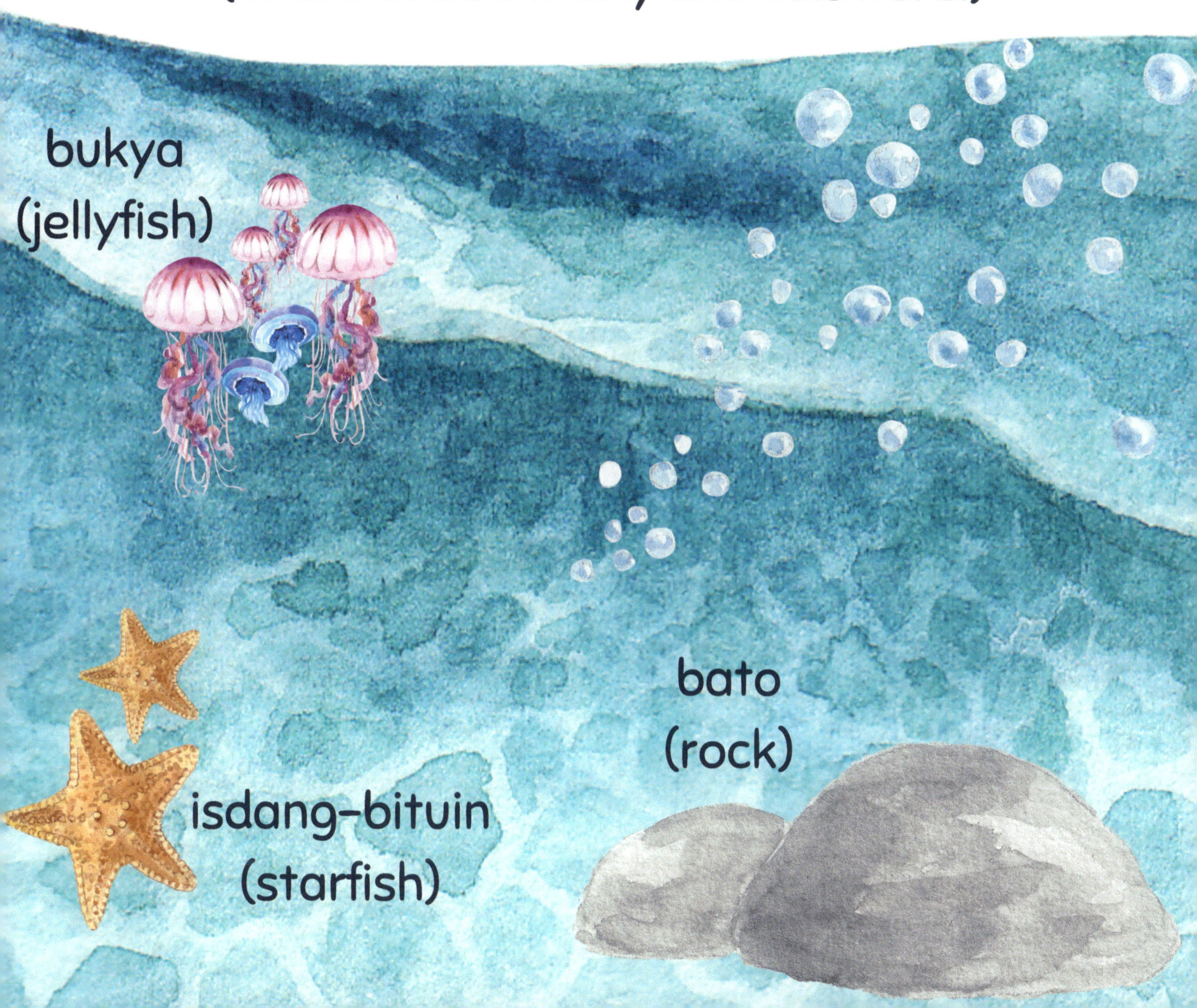

Tan-awa!
(Look!)

The langit (sky) is changing!
Do you see the langam (birds)?

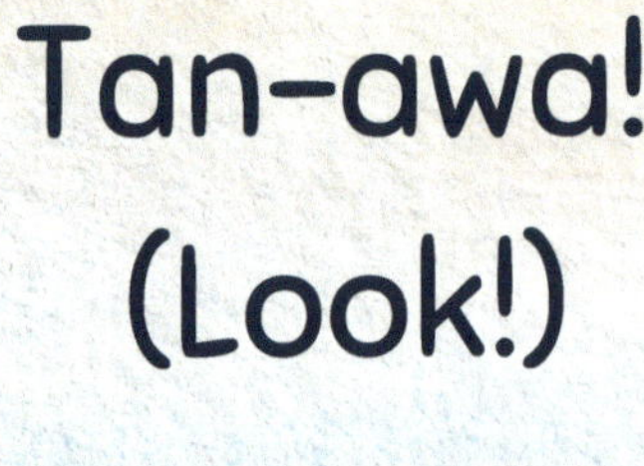

Moadto na ang barko.
(The boat is leaving.)

Mag-ulan ba?
(Will it rain?)

No, it looks like the
clouds are moving.

Nalingaw kaayo ko sa dagat pero kinahanglan nga kita mobiya.

(I had such a good time at the beach, but it's time to go.)

Wait!
Kinahanglan ta mokaon og aiskrim.
(We must eat ice cream.)

So many yummy flavors.
Unsa man imong paborito?
(Which one is your favorite?

Pagpauli na ta!
(Time to go home.)

Magkita ta sa sunod.
(See you next time!)

The Philippines is an island country in Southeast Asia in the western Pacific Ocean. It is an archipelago consisting of more than 7000 islands.

There are around 182 living languages in the Philippines.

There are 30 languages that constitute the Bisayan language family. Our family is from Bohol, Cebu, Cagayan de Oro, and Camp Phillips.

About the Author

Catherine Gamolo Agopcan is a Financial Educator and Sustainability Advocate. She moved to the US at the age of 9.

This book was written to help her daughter learn more about Filipino culture and language. She wants to make sure the next generation takes pride in their background and heritage as Filipino people.